Acting Edition

Real American Dinner Party & Other Short Plays

by Jen Silverman

‖SAMUEL FRENCH‖

Copyright © 2021 by Jen Silverman
All Rights Reserved

REAL AMERICAN DINNER PARTY & OTHER SHORT PLAYS is fully protected under the copyright laws of the United States of America, the British Commonwealth, including Canada, and all member countries of the Berne Convention for the Protection of Literary and Artistic Works, the Universal Copyright Convention, and/or the World Trade Organization conforming to the Agreement on Trade Related Aspects of Intellectual Property Rights. All rights, including professional and amateur stage productions, recitation, lecturing, public reading, motion picture, radio broadcasting, television, online/digital production, and the rights of translation into foreign languages are strictly reserved.

ISBN 978-0-573-70939-5

www.concordtheatricals.com
www.concordtheatricals.co.uk

FOR PRODUCTION INQUIRIES

UNITED STATES AND CANADA
info@concordtheatricals.com
1-866-979-0447

UNITED KINGDOM AND EUROPE
licensing@concordtheatricals.co.uk
020-7054-7200

Each title is subject to availability from Concord Theatricals Corp., depending upon country of performance. Please be aware that *REAL AMERICAN DINNER PARTY & OTHER SHORT PLAYS* may not be licensed by Concord Theatricals Corp. in your territory. Professional and amateur producers should contact the nearest Concord Theatricals Corp. office or licensing partner to verify availability.

CAUTION: Professional and amateur producers are hereby warned that *REAL AMERICAN DINNER PARTY & OTHER SHORT PLAYS* is subject to a licensing fee. The purchase, renting, lending or use of this book does not constitute a license to perform this title(s), which license must be obtained from Concord Theatricals Corp. prior to any performance. Performance of this title(s) without a license is a violation of federal law and may subject the producer and/or presenter of such performances to civil penalties. Both amateurs and professionals considering a production are strongly advised to apply to the appropriate agent before starting rehearsals, advertising, or booking a theatre. A licensing fee must be paid whether the title(s) is presented for charity or gain and whether or not admission is charged. Professional/Stock licensing fees are quoted upon application to Concord Theatricals Corp.

This work is published by Samuel French, an imprint of Concord Theatricals Corp.

No one shall make any changes in this title(s) for the purpose of production. No part of this book may be reproduced, stored in a retrieval system, scanned, uploaded, or transmitted in any form, by any means, now known or yet to be invented, including mechanical, electronic, digital, photocopying, recording, videotaping, or otherwise, without the prior written permission of the publisher. No one shall share this title(s), or any part of this title(s), through any social media or file hosting websites.

For all inquiries regarding motion picture, television, online/digital and other media rights, please contact Concord Theatricals Corp.

MUSIC AND THIRD-PARTY MATERIALS USE NOTE

Licensees are solely responsible for obtaining formal written permission from copyright owners to use copyrighted music and/or other copyrighted third-party materials (e.g., artworks, logos) in the performance of this play and are strongly cautioned to do so. If no such permission is obtained by the licensee, then the licensee must use only original music and materials that the licensee owns and controls. Licensees are solely responsible and liable for clearances of all third-party copyrighted materials, including without limitation music, and shall indemnify the copyright owners of the play(s) and their licensing agent, Concord Theatricals Corp., against any costs, expenses, losses and liabilities arising from the use of such copyrighted third-party materials by licensees. For music, please contact the appropriate music licensing authority in your territory for the rights to any incidental music.

IMPORTANT BILLING AND CREDIT REQUIREMENTS

If you have obtained performance rights to this title, please refer to your licensing agreement for important billing and credit requirements.

TABLE OF CONTENTS

The Visitations 1
Hippos of the Eastern Enclosure 11
Ubu Anew (A Play for Strange People) 39
Your Mother in the Night Sky 79
Real American Dinner Party 91

A note on the short plays that follow:

The spacing on the page is a gesture toward indicating rhythm and how thoughts change, morph, contradict each other, escalate, or get supplanted by other thoughts as we talk. The line breaks do not indicate a beat or pause except where written.

(Sentences inside parentheses) are spoken, but indicate a side-thought or shift away from the main thought.

The Visitations

THE VISITATIONS was commissioned by Weston Playhouse under Artistic Director Susanna Gellert. This piece was produced in Weston's One Room Festival in August 2020, directed by Mike Donahue and performed by Dana Delany. (Though the character is also named Dana, this monologue is not autobiographical.)

CHARACTERS

DANA – charming, cheeky, lonely

AUTHOR'S NOTE

This was originally written to be performed on a Zoom screen. This monologue should work well both in a digital format or on a stage. If performed on a stage, the magic trick at the end can be altered to better suit live, physical space.

(**DANA.** *On the other side of a Zoom window.*)

(*She leans close to the camera. She does this for an unsettling beat, then:*)

DANA. Sorry, I'm just trying to see if there's anyone else there.

I mean behind me, in the sort of...

Someone I can't see.

(*A quick glance around her own space.*)

Sorry, I just – I'm never sure if he's listening or not.

I don't know what the rules are – like, how far away does he have to be, to be within earshot? You know? I can tell when he's in the room –

or if I walk into the room and he's *just* left, I can tell that sometimes –

there's this way the hair on my arms sort of...lifts, or

also the back of the neck? that prickle? –

Or my eyes will tear up sometimes –

(which at first I thought was allergies

even though it was March, it was mid-March when I started staying in here all day

and there wasn't exactly anything *blooming*, not in an aggressive spring-like way)

– but you tell yourself these stories

because you want to think – well, I mean, it's *my* house.

I didn't sign up for someone else to be in it!

Of course someone else lived there first, someone had it before me, but now it's *mine* and it just seems really...aggressive... to have to share.

And then, you know, things escalated.

The crashing upstairs, and I'd go upstairs, and no one would be there or

all the times I'd close the window and then I'd come in later and the window would be open or

you know, I would put something down and turn around and it would be gone

and later I'd find it somewhere I absolutely never would put it

(he seems to have a real fascination with my *things*)

or the time the Apple TV box just *jumped* off the table

– every time I would try to watch this one show – I won't say which one, but –

the Apple TV box would just *fling* itself to the ground

in an absolute *rejection* of my desires and my tastes

and finally I gave up and now we just watch PBS all day

and things are quiet when we're watching PBS

either he's so bored he just abandons the room to me or he likes PBS –

(I can't *always* tell when he's here, I do want to clarify that part,

sometimes he makes it quite clear but other times I just have no idea.)

So anyway.
Obviously I said to myself: Oh, you have a ghost.
I mean it isn't *rocket science*, you just add up all the things and you go:
Oh, it's a ghost!

And then the dreams started.
I haven't told *anyone* this.

>   *(Beat.* **DANA** *considers not telling.)*

>   *(But it's just so good!)*

Nobody wants to hear about anybody else's dreams so
I'm not going to bore you with the details but
let me just say…

they are *sexual*.
In nature.

Eros
you know?

who was it – someone said –
Eros, the bittersweet.

Actually I think that's a title – I think it's an Anne Carson book –

anyway, I told my sister and she said that she might characterize them
as *visitations*, which
you know, is not something *I* had been saying but
they are a bit more vivid than just…a dream.
For example –
I'm really not going to go into detail here but –
let me just say,

Elijah
(that's his name, as far as I can make out)
Elijah Elliott
(he built this as a bungalow in 1920 – I've done research!)

Elijah

(the owner before me did a reno, Eli hates the new part of the house)

Eli

(won't even go in it, or if he does, it's just to throw things)

I think we fucked.

(Didn't quite mean to say that.)

I think we –

Made love.

It's not the kind of relationship I planned to have but also

the risk of transmission

– of *anything*, really –

is very low.

(Glancing around for a Presence.)

Relationship feels like maybe I'm jumping the gun a little bit.

Just – you know – he made –

Contact.

First Contact.

(That's a movie.)

(Beat, in a rush:)

I was in bed, it was late at night – and raining, I remember that it had been raining all evening – and I had been reading *The Paris Review* which is really the only magazine of any kind that I read anymore, and I started to doze off so I turned off the light and then all of a sudden, I became aware of a hand that was... on my thigh. Gently resting there. *On top* of the sheet, I should say, so there was a thin thin layer of fabric between his hand and my thigh, and I know we're in a moment where men can't just put their grabby little hands on our thighs anymore, but also I don't know how that applies to dead ones, exactly, and also I can't say that it was unwelcome, in the exact moment in which he introduced the idea.

    (Beat.)

And things just...progressed from there.

And could I see him? No. But could I feel him? Yes – And honestly, when your eyes are closed, how much of a difference is there between somebody you *can* see and somebody you *can't*?

Anyway, this is all to say: we think we know what we want but maybe we don't.

We think we know our futures and

our politics and

our science and

our bodies and

our houses, our places of refuge and

maybe we just don't know a goddamn thing about any of that stuff?

You know?

That's the conclusion that I'm coming to.

But also? It's very likely that I'm losing my mind.

    (And then.)

    (In the square of screen still visible behind **DANA***, something happens.)*

    (A sign of haunting.)

    (A magic trick.)

    (Maybe a coffee cup levitates from a side-table.)

(Maybe a book carries itself across the frame.)

*(Maybe a painting, hanging behind **DANA** on the wall, suddenly tips to the right.)*

(Maybe a ball bounces down the stairs.)

*(Whatever it is, it is a sudden and unmistakable sign of presence. **DANA** is not alone in her home.)*

(And she feels it!)

(As she turns – an eagerness.)

Hello?

(The screen goes black.)

End of Play

Hippos of the Eastern Enclosure

HIPPOS OF THE EASTERN ENCLOSURE was commissioned by Clubbed Thumb under Artistic Director Maria Striar. It was produced in the 2017 Winterworks Festival and directed by Christina Roussos as part of Clubbed Thumb's Directing Fellowship, led by Anne Kauffman and Ken Rus Schmoll. The cast for that production was as follows:

ELLY	Renata Friedman
JACOB	Paco Tolson
SYLVIA	Kristin Villanueva
LARGE (A HIPPO)	Heather Simms
SMALL (A HIPPO)	Polly Lee
SPOTTY (A HIPPO)	Layla Khosh

CHARACTERS

ELLY – socially strange but very candid
JACOB – sweet but skittish
SYLVIA – curious and unafraid
LARGE (A HIPPO) – fierce and driven
SMALL (A HIPPO) – also fierce, scared of Large
SPOTTY (A HIPPO) – meek, she got bullied as a baby hippo

These characters can be played by any race or ethnicity. But please avoid any casting scenario where all the humans are played by actors of one race and all the hippos are played by actors of another.

SETTING

A zoo: the front office and the hippo enclosure

We need very few props. The space should be nearly bare, theatrical, fluid. We move quickly between office and hippo enclosure. This moves quickly.

For Dane Laffrey

1.

(The front office of a zoo.)

*(**ELLY** sits at the desk. **JACOB** enters.)*

JACOB. They started.

ELLY. Huh?

JACOB. All at once.

ELLY. Oh god.

JACOB. All in sync.

ELLY. Are you serious?

JACOB. It's a mess in there.

ELLY. I bet.

JACOB. Who's on clean-up?

ELLY. You.

JACOB. Me? Nah.

ELLY. You. You're on clean-up. You're on feeding, you're on everything.

JACOB. Me?? Nah.

ELLY. Thanksgiving, dude. There's you. There's me.

JACOB. Well.

ELLY. Yeah?

JACOB. There's… I don't wanna sound…but there's you.

ELLY. Uh-huh.

JACOB. There's me. *And* there's you.

ELLY. I'm on desk duty.

JACOB. Who says?

ELLY. I've been here longer. I know about the paperwork. The order forms.

JACOB. I know how to order things.

ELLY. Just because you got an Amazon habit doesn't mean you know about the *paperwork*. I know about paperwork. I got the paperwork. You got the other stuff, right now.

JACOB. *(Hopefully: "So there's a later?")* "Right now"?

ELLY. When I'm done, I'll come out, I'll do the lions, I'll do the giraffes –

JACOB. When are you gonna be done?

ELLY. Not right now.

JACOB. You could do the hippos, and I could do the lions and giraffes.

ELLY. Nope.

JACOB. Come on!

ELLY. You got hippos.

JACOB. They're bleeding.

ELLY. I know, you said.

JACOB. Their periods are all –

ELLY. I know!

JACOB. I don't even have sisters!

ELLY. Do you have a girlfriend?

JACOB. Yeah.

ELLY. Well. It's like that.

JACOB. My *girlfriend* doesn't –

ELLY. She does. Oh she does, my young friend. Yes she does.

> *(Beat. It becomes apparent to* **JACOB** *and to* **ELLY** *and to the rest of us that* **JACOB** *does not want to think about his girlfriend's period.)*

JACOB. I didn't know hippos even did that shit.

ELLY. These ones.

JACOB. Okay.

ELLY. Don't you read *any* of the materials? They're special.

JACOB. They're hippos.

ELLY. They're a breed, like a special – ugh don't you read?

JACOB. I read.

ELLY. We give all new employees pamphlets and instruction sheets and *manuals* –

JACOB. I read the manuals!

ELLY. – And they all say that the hippos in the eastern enclosure are a special breed of hippo, and they require different things from the other hippos, their *diet* is even a different diet, and then once a month – ugh. You should've read all of this.

JACOB. I guess *that page*, okay, maybe somehow I missed *that page* –

ELLY. Okay. Well. So. You didn't read it, so.

> *(Beat.)*

JACOB. So you want me to like. Go in there.

ELLY. Uh-huh.

JACOB. Like into the enclosure. With them.

ELLY. I mean. Yes.

JACOB. While they're...?

ELLY. Menstruating.

You can say the word.

(Beat. Trying to make a bargain:)

JACOB. I'll do the jackals *and* the weird ugly monkeys.

ELLY. I know.

JACOB. No, I mean – I'll do those *in addition* to the lions and the giraffes.

If you do the hippos.

ELLY. Jacob.

JACOB. *And* the lemurs.

ELLY. Jacob!

JACOB. *(Desperate.)* And the naked mole rats!!

ELLY. JACOB, THE NAKED MOLE RATS DO NOT REQUIRE ANYTHING FROM YOU.

*(Beat, they stare at each other. **ELLY** takes a breath.)*

The hippos have needs. Are you gonna do your job and respond to their needs?

(Beat.)

*(**JACOB** picks up his mop and walks out.)*

2.

(The **HIPPOS. LARGE, SMALL,** *and* **SPOTTY.** *They are all lady-hippos.)*

(It's possible they stand behind the low wall of a hippo enclosure, so we can't see whether or not they're menstruating.)

LARGE. I heard she got moved to the western enclosure.

SMALL. No!!

LARGE. She like, does that smarmy-charmy thing –

SMALL. Oh my god totally –

LARGE. Where she like, gets really close to the glass –

SMALL. So they can all see her, so like, the little kids –

LARGE. And the photos!

SMALL. They all take photos!

LARGE. And she eats it up.

SMALL. Tries to pretend like she doesn't even notice –

LARGE. "Oh, cameras?? Are those for me?"

SMALL. But it gives her LIFE.

LARGE. What a cunt.

SMALL. That fucking caribou. I can*not* believe she landed the western enclosure.

SPOTTY. Is that good?

*(**LARGE** and **SMALL** look at her.)*

LARGE. Is it good? Is it *good*?

SMALL. It's the *best*.

LARGE. Have *you* ever been in the western enclosure?

SPOTTY. No.

LARGE. So.

SPOTTY. I'm new here.

LARGE. ...We know.

SMALL. It's – trust us – it's the best.

SPOTTY. Have *you* guys ever been in the western enclosure?

LARGE. No. Because *we* don't bat our fuckin' eyelashes for the cameras.

SMALL. We've only ever been in the eastern enclosure.

SPOTTY. So how do you know the western enclosure is the best?

SMALL. We hear.

LARGE. We've heard.

SMALL. We hear things.

LARGE. That fucking caribou.

(Beat.)

SPOTTY. *(Re:* **JACOB.***)* Is the skinny one running late?

LARGE. What a loser.

SMALL. It's never on time.

LARGE. The girl's better.

SMALL. Is it a girl?

SPOTTY. I can't tell them apart.

LARGE. It's a girl.

SPOTTY. How do you know?

LARGE. It's always on time.

(The **HIPPOS** *laugh.)*

SMALL. But seriously though, you know what I heard?

LARGE & SPOTTY. *(Eager.)* What!

SMALL. I heard the giraffe in the southern enclosure?

LARGE & SPOTTY. Yeeees?

SMALL. She booked a commercial.

LARGE & SPOTTY. No!!

SMALL. SHE DID SHE BOOKED A COMMERCIAL.

LARGE. *Fuck* her.

SPOTTY. ...Isn't that good?

LARGE. "Good"?

SPOTTY. For her?

SMALL. *Fuck* her.

LARGE. Where's my commercial?

SPOTTY. I just meant –

LARGE. Where's my goddamn commercial? Where's my close-up? Where's my *publicity campaign*?

SMALL. Preach!

SPOTTY. *(Timid.)* I'd like one too.

LARGE. Well you don't have one. And you wanna know *why* you don't have one?

SPOTTY. ...Why?

SMALL. Because the fucking giraffe does.

LARGE. She took it from you. Essentially.

SPOTTY. But I don't even know her.

LARGE. Listen. This is a scarcity economy. Say there's a commercial. Say there's a residency in the western enclosure. Say there's extra feed! You could get those things. Or somebody else could beat you out. There's one slot. There's one candidate. Who's it gonna be?

SMALL. There's two types of creatures in this world.

LARGE. You –

SMALL. – And your competition.

(**LARGE** and **SMALL** *nod at each other.*)

SPOTTY. But don't you think we're doing okay?

SMALL. Do you want to do okay, or do you want to do THE BEST?

(*They look at* **SPOTTY** *very seriously.*)

SPOTTY. I would sort of just like everybody to have enough.

LARGE. She's basically a communist.

(*The two* **HIPPOS** *turn away.* **SPOTTY** *is forlorn.*)

LARGE. Goddamn it.

SMALL. What?

LARGE. Got my...

SMALL. Oh! Oh wow. Is it time?

LARGE. Snuck up on me.

SMALL. (*A new realization.*) Oh!

LARGE. You too?

SMALL. That time of the month.

(*They look at* **SPOTTY**.)

SPOTTY. I guess I'm out of sync with you guys.

LARGE. I guess so.

(**LARGE** and **SMALL** *turn their backs.*)

3.

*(**ELLY** in the office. Paperwork. Enter **SYLVIA**.)*

ELLY. Can I help you?

SYLVIA. I'm looking for Jacob?

ELLY. He's out with the hippos right now.

SYLVIA. Oh...I thought his shift would be over?

ELLY. We're understaffed.

They all started their cycle on the same day.

SYLVIA. "Cycle"?

*(**ELLY** looks at her hard.)*

Oh.

(Beat.)

I'm Jacob's girlfriend. And the thing is...

Here's the thing, I thought Jacob was getting off work hours ago?

Because his family is about to show up at our apartment. For Thanksgiving.

In say, possibly half an hour, his entire clan will descend.

And Jacob is supposed to be home helping me prepare...and he's not? And I called him and his phone is dead, because his phone is always dead.

So.

I was wondering if you could call him for me.

(Beat.)

ELLY. Well. We're understaffed, like I mentioned...

SYLVIA. Uh-huh.

ELLY. So it's me and Jacob. Here. For the foreseeable future.

SYLVIA. "The foreseeable future…"

ELLY. Until we close.

SYLVIA. And when do you close?

ELLY. Say, eight. Seven-thirty or eight. It'll be a little more up to our discretion than usual today, so say seven-thirty.

SYLVIA. But it's Thanksgiving!!

ELLY. I know, that's why we're understaffed.

SYLVIA. Why is the zoo open until seven-thirty on Thanksgiving??

ELLY. Because people eat their meals, they overstuff themselves with their oversize meals, and then they need to take a walk. They need to take a walk with their families, so that they can get some kind of respite from looking at and talking to their families. They need to take this walk, and come look at these animals instead of each other, and try not to say all the things they are trying not to say, and instead they get to say things like, "Oh wow a bear," and, "Oh wow an otter," and, "Oh wow, the hippos are bleeding everywhere."

SYLVIA. Bleeding??

ELLY. Their cycle.

SYLVIA. OH. Right.

ELLY. Right, so, that is why we are open until say, eight p.m. on Thanksgiving.

(Beat.)

SYLVIA. Where is Jacob, exactly?

ELLY. "Exactly," I don't know "exactly."

If he's finished with the hippos, he's probably at the caribou.

SYLVIA. You guys have caribou?

ELLY. In the western enclosure, if you want to check it out.

She's very photogenic, the caribou.

SYLVIA. *(Beat.)* Listen, I can't go back to the apartment if Jacob's folks are coming and Jacob isn't there.

ELLY. Why not?

(Beat.)

SYLVIA. ...Are you not doing Thanksgiving?

ELLY. I don't like major holidays.

SYLVIA. You...?

ELLY. Humans gather. Humans eat. Humans force food into their faces and modify their behavior for each other. But these modifications won't stick. The dishonesty of it makes me so depressed. I used to participate in major holidays, and then the day after I would be so sad that I couldn't get out of bed. I would just lie in bed and stare at the ceiling and I would think: *horrible horrible human*. I would think about all the ways I lied with my mouth and my eyes and my thoughts and my intentions, and I would feel ugly. So I've stopped doing major holidays, and I have to tell you I feel a lot better.

(Beat.)

SYLVIA. I should try that.

ELLY. Maybe. I don't know you, so I don't know, but it helped me a lot.

SYLVIA. No, I should definitely try that.

Jacob's mom hates me?

ELLY. Oh.

SYLVIA. Yeah his mom *loved* his ex. Like: Loved.

And…I'm not his ex. So she hates me.

ELLY. That seems counterproductive.

SYLVIA. I mean. That wasn't the word I'd pick, but it works.

ELLY. Animals don't participate in this kind of thing. I don't know if you look at animals that much, but I do. I do all the time. They eat when they're hungry and they sleep when they want to sleep and they're aggressive when they want to be aggressive. They don't modify their behaviors out of politeness, although they might in the interests of survival. And when a mate dies, or is banished, or leaves…they just find another mate. You know? They regroup.

SYLVIA. I don't really watch animals all that much, so…

ELLY. You and Jacob regrouped.

SYLVIA. *(Now she likes this idea.)* I guess we did. Yeah!

ELLY. You regrouped!

SYLVIA. We regrouped!

ELLY. You regrouped and in many other animal societies, you would be welcomed.

SYLVIA. I would be?

ELLY. In many. Not all. But many.

(Beat. Warmer, more comfortable. They sit.)

SYLVIA. Like which ones?

ELLY. Like hippos.

SYLVIA. Hippos?

ELLY. Hippos are very welcoming.

4.

(The hippo enclosure.)

(The **HIPPOS** *remain behind the low wall.)*

*(***LARGE** *is beside herself with outrage.)*

LARGE. – And they put her ass on stage!

SMALL & SPOTTY. No!

LARGE. They did! They did! First female warthog to ever perform on a *stage*.

SPOTTY. That's amazing.

LARGE. Are you kidding? Are you kidding me? WHERE'S MY FUCKING STAGE?

SPOTTY. I only meant –

SMALL. They just gave it to her because she's a warthog.

LARGE. I know! I know!

SMALL. She's not any better than you. She's just a warthog.

LARGE. Well I know that!

SPOTTY. Don't you guys think it's really important to put warthogs' stories onstage?

*(***LARGE** *and* **SMALL** *look at her with disdain.)*

LARGE. More important than *my* story?

SPOTTY. I didn't say *more* important, but just sort of like… her story is important too. And nobody talks about her story that much. So maybe it's culturally important for us, even though it's not about us.

(Beat.)

LARGE. Nope.

SMALL. No.

LARGE. Are you crazy?

SMALL. She's crazy.

LARGE. That's just crazy.

SMALL. If it's not my story, it's not important to me.

LARGE. What she said.

(Beat.)

SPOTTY. Sorry.

(Beat.)

LARGE. You know what really burns me up?

SMALL. What?

LARGE. Yesterday this family was in here, ugly little kid, smushy face –

SMALL. Oh yeah I saw them –

LARGE. Walks right up to the enclosure, sticks its smushy face right over the wall –

SMALL. – Oh yeah –

LARGE. Looks straight at me, says, "Look at the weird cow, Momma."

SMALL. Jesus.

LARGE. I know.

SMALL. Oh man.

LARGE. I know!

SMALL. What a fucking world.

LARGE. I KNOW!

SPOTTY. I thought it was funny?

LARGE. *(Ignoring her.)* If my ass had a show booked, do you know what that fat little waste of space would've said?

SMALL. "Look at the hippo!"

LARGE. "Momma, look at the famous fucking hippo!"

(Beat.)

SPOTTY. I thought it was kind of funny?

LARGE. You would.

SMALL. You know what we need in this world?

LARGE. *(Aimed at* **SPOTTY.***)* Some self-respect, to start with.

SMALL. And a TV spot.

LARGE. And an agent.

SMALL. And some goddamn royalties.

LARGE. And the western enclosure.

SMALL. *Definitely* the western enclosure. And some Advil.

LARGE. Advil?

SMALL. *(Re: cramps.)* You know.

LARGE. I don't do Advil.

SMALL. You don't?

LARGE. I wanna be in touch with my pain. Source of my power.

SMALL. Oh.

LARGE. Font of my female flow.

SMALL. I never thought of it like that.

LARGE. Magnetic epicenter of raw poetry.

SPOTTY. Poetry?

LARGE. Slam poetry.

> (**LARGE** *takes a step and clears her throat.*)
>
> (**SMALL** *draws back respectfully.*)

SMALL. Ooh watch out.

SPOTTY. Is she okay??

SMALL. She's going to do a poem.

> (**JACOB** *enters. He's carrying a mop.*)
>
> (*He looks at the* **HIPPOS**.)
>
> (*They all look at him. He is too scared of what is behind the low wall. He can't deal.*)

JACOB. Oh man.

> (*He exits.*)
>
> (*The* **HIPPOS** *whip themselves up into a freestyling frenzy. This performance is the most united front we have ever seen from them, and in its own way, it is communal and strong and perfect. The other* **HIPPOS** *might clap and stomp and beatbox as backup for whichever* **HIPPO** *is rapping.*)

HIPPOS. Hey!

Hey!

Hey!

Hey!

LARGE.
FEMALE INFINITY, FEMALE MASCULINITY
FEMININE AMBITION IS IGNITION FOR THE ENEMY
MAGNA CARTA CHARTER SIGN THE PARTA IT THAT'S MEANT FOR ME

RELEGATE ME CUZ YOU HATE ME BUT YOU CAN'T CONTAIN MY ENERGY
I'M A VOLCANO! I'M A RAINBOW! I'M INSANE THOUGH!
I'VE GONE POSTAL! I'M STILL LOCAL! I'M A STAR THOUGH!
THESE RAGING RED TIDES BRING ME POWER
THESE RAGING RED TIDES BRING ME POWER
THESE RAGING RED TIDES BRING ME POWER.

HIPPOS. Hey!

Hey!

Hey!

Hey!

SMALL.

HIPPO-HOPPIN' DON'T BE STOPPIN' YOU DON'T KNOW WHEN I MIGHT DROP IN

I'M CHARTIN' CHARTS THAT YOU'RE NOT TOPPIN', GOODY-BAG LIKE MARY POPPINS

HIPPOS GONNA STAGE A STOMP-IN, WORK ME LORD LIKE JANIS JOPLIN

TIME AFTER TIME LIKE CINDY LAUPER, I'M THE PRINCE AND YOU'RE THE PAUPER.

WESTERN ENCLOSURE? IN FORECLOSURE! CARIBOU DIE OF EXPOSURE!

NEVER HEARD A HERD OF HIPPOS? LIKE DYNAMITE RIGHT BY A ZIPPO!

HIPPOS.

THESE RAGING RED TIDES BRING ME POWER!

*(**SPOTTY** steps forward. She has never participated before, but this feels really exciting and good!)*

SPOTTY.

SOCIALISM IS A PRISM, RAINBOW GLOW YOU SEE WE'RE RISEN

SPOTTY.
>DIVIDE AND CONQUER WILLY WONKA TONKA TRUCKS CREATE A PRISON
>CHOCOLATE FACTORY TAKE A WHACK AT ME, MEN IN SUITS IN GROUPS ATTACKIN' ME!
>I DON'T NEED THESE TRACKERS TRACKIN' ME! ALL I NEED IS LADIES BACKIN' ME!
>SISTERS ASSISTIN' – INTERMISSION! – CHANEL PRECISION MAKES ME GLISTEN
>WATCH ME WORK WITH RAW PRECISION, ALL THAT'S MISSIN'? MALE PERMISSION!

HIPPOS.
>THESE RAGING RED TIDES BRING ME POWER
>THESE RAGING RED TIDES BRING ME POWER
>THESE RAGING RED TIDES BRING ME POWER!

>>*(The* **HIPPOS** *totally lose it. They applaud themselves.* **LARGE** *and* **SPOTTY** *high-five or back-clap. This is a gorgeous moment of unity.)*

5.

(The office.)

(ELLY and SYLVIA are more relaxed. Mid-convo:)

SYLVIA. What about you?

ELLY. I was bullied as a child.

SYLVIA. Okay...

ELLY. Usually when I say that, people say, "That explains everything."

SYLVIA. A *lot*, but not *everything*.

ELLY. What else... I had a pet frog.

We were close.

SYLVIA. Uh-huh?

(SYLVIA waits for there to be more. There isn't more. ELLY realizes SYLVIA wants more.)

ELLY. It died.

SYLVIA. I'm sorry to hear that.

ELLY. I've had a lot of despair since then, I guess.

SYLVIA. How long ago...?

ELLY. About fifteen, sixteen years.

SYLVIA. ...Oh.

I'm so sorry for your loss.

ELLY. *(Means it.)* Thank you.

(JACOB comes in, with his mop.)

SYLVIA. Jay!

JACOB. What are you doing here?

ELLY. How are the hippos?

SYLVIA. I came looking for you.

JACOB. My whole family is supposed to be at our apartment right now!

SYLVIA. Yeah did you think I was gonna face them alone?

ELLY. Did you take care of the hippos?

JACOB. Look, we're understaffed –

SYLVIA. Yeah I heard –

JACOB. So I'm running a little late.

SYLVIA. Well then me too, I'm running a little late too.

ELLY. You skipped the hippos.

>   *(Beat.)*
>
>   (**SYLVIA** *looks at* **JACOB** *accusingly.*)

SYLVIA. Jay!

ELLY. Didn't you!

SYLVIA. Jay did you skip the hippos??

JACOB. Guys.

ELLY. It's been hours!

SYLVIA. They're probably waiting for you.

JACOB. Guys, I couldn't.

  I couldn't do the hippos.

SYLVIA. Oh Jesus.

ELLY. Jacob! It's your job!

JACOB. I did the caribou and the giraffes and the lions and the warthog and I did the naked mole rats even though you said the naked mole rats don't need anything from me – you were wrong by the way – and I did the ostriches and I did the puma and I did the mangy monkeys.

ELLY. But not the hippos.

SYLVIA. You didn't think the hippos deserved some help either?

JACOB. You guys! It's just – ugh. It's just a sensitive moment for me to go in there.

I tried, okay, I stood outside the enclosure and I just...

I just...

ELLY. You're scared.

SYLVIA. He *is* scared.

JACOB. I'm not scared!

ELLY & SYLVIA. *(To each other.)* He's scared.

ELLY. *(A concession.)* ...It's okay.

We'll all go.

6.

(The hippo enclosure.)

*(***SYLVIA**, **JACOB**, *and* **ELLY** *enter.)*

SYLVIA. That one is amazing.

JACOB. Which one?

SYLVIA. The weird spotty one.

ELLY. Oh yeah, she's new.

> *(***SYLVIA** *approaches the hippo pen. The* **HIPPOS** *all turn their attention to her.)*

LARGE. What's that.

SPOTTY. It's a new one.

LARGE. It's another girl one.

SMALL. It's looking at us!

> *(As they realize where her attention is directed...)*

LARGE. ...It's looking at HER!!

SPOTTY. ...Hi.

Oh hi,

oh hello.

> *(***LARGE** *and* **SMALL** *turn on* **SPOTTY**, *an accusatory stare.)*
>
> *(But* **SPOTTY** *doesn't notice them.)*
>
> *(She is basking in* **SYLVIA***'s stare.* **SPOTTY** *has entirely forgotten where she is, who she is with, sisterhood and socialism be damned...she turns and poses and finds her light beneath the glorious beaming eye of celebrity.)*

LARGE. Hey!

SMALL. Over here!

LARGE. Hey look at me too!

SMALL. Hey I'm a star!

LARGE. In the making!

SMALL. Hello?

LARGE. Hey there!

SYLVIA. *(Re:* **SPOTTY.***)* She's a natural.

>*(A moment in which time freezes.)*
>
>*(And* **SPOTTY** *steps out toward us.)*
>
>*(The lights change. They bathe her in the warm golden glow of success. She speaks to us directly, with absolute charm and confidence. This is the voice of success.)*
>
>*(It sounds very different from yester-***SPOTTY.***)*

SPOTTY. I used to be a nobody – like you, I imagine. This was before I was who I now am. This was before my days here in the western enclosure. This was before the ad campaign – or the documentary series – or the autobiographical children's book. Well. Let me amend that first statement. I used to be a nobody – but perhaps I was not *quite* like you. After all, I attracted greatness. I coaxed it to me.

Listen. I'll tell you something – and this is for free: The thing about success is that, if it comes, it is a singular pursuit. It comes to you, the individual. It does not come to the person to your right. Nor to your left. Like the hand of God, it lands on you.

People say: *When you get to the top, send the elevator back down.*

I say: I didn't take the elevator up here, I took the stairs.

People say: *A rising tide lifts all boats.*

I say: If you stack enough bodies in the water, the tide goes up.

People say: *United we stand, divided we fall.*

I say: There is no "we" in warrior. That's a WA.

There's not enough to go around.

But the little bit there is?

That's for me.

>(**SPOTTY** *smiles at us.*)
>
>(*Her smile is ice-cold.*)
>
>(*Blackout.*)

End of Play

Ubu Anew
(A Play for Strange People)

An early version of *UBU ANEW (A PLAY FOR STRANGE PEOPLE)* was commissioned by InterAct Theatre Company under Artistic Director Seth Rozin for PAPAYA (Pennsylvania Performing Arts for Young Audiences) under the artistic leadership of Whit McLaughlin.

CHARACTERS

UBU – overconfident and emotionally fragile but oddly charming
MA UBU – increasingly ambitious
WENZ JR. – slippery, sharp
THE BABY WENZ – an optimist and an innocent
MR. WENZ – an old-fashioned but decent man
   Can also play: **SAD POSTMAN / SAD DESTITUTE PERSON**
ROSE WENZ – concerned with what others think
   Can also play: **SAD TEACHER / HILLARY CLINTON**

AUTHOR'S NOTES

Casting: It is possible to double-cast the play, in which case the cast size is six. It is also possible to ignore the double-casting suggestions above and have a larger cast. Characters can be played by actors of any race or gender identity.

Set & Props: Very minimal. What is most important is keeping a tight, fast pace and fluid transitions from scene to scene. The more this feels simple, economical, and theatrical, the better. The only props that are genuinely important are: a grotesque number of Pixy Stix (don't stint), and Super Soakers filled with colored dye (don't be scared).

Acting Style: Treat these scenes like very serious naturalism. No matter how absurd or strange it gets, the characters are utterly sincere in what they believe and say. There's no room for commentary or parody.

Music: Feel free to use your own music for the sung lyrics. Music must be original or in the public domain.

1. A Song

(**UBU** *walks onstage. He might wear grubby Chuck Taylors. He sings a very simple song.*)

(*It starts like a folk song.*)

UBU.
CHAOS MAKES SOME PEOPLE UNEASY
BUT NOT ME!
I WANT EVERYTHING TO FALL APART
ALL THE TIME!
I DON'T EVEN LIKE IT WHEN SONGS RHYME
BECAUSE THAT IMPLIES ORDER
AND HONESTLY, I HATE ORDER.

I AM GOING TO BE THE KING SOMEDAY
NO MATTER WHAT!
I'M NEVER GOING TO CHANGE MY BOXER SHORTS
AND YOU CAN'T MAKE ME!
I WILL DRINK EVERYTHING WITH A STRAW
REGARDLESS OF WHAT I AM DRINKING
AND IF I WANT GUMMY WORMS, I WILL HAVE THEM.

PEOPLE SAY THAT KNOWLEDGE IS POWER
THAT'S STUPID: POWER IS POWER.
PEOPLE SAY THAT THERE'S NO "I" IN TEAM
THAT'S CORRECT: BUT THERE'S AN "I" IN *RIGHT NOW!!*

(*The song becomes aggro and shouty.*)

GET YOUR CHANGE.ORG
OUT OF MY FACE!
GET YOUR KICKSTARTER

UBU.
>OUT OF MY FACE!
>I DON'T CARE ABOUT THE COMMON GOOD
>SO GET OUT OF MY FACE!
>I JUST WANT TO BE HAPPY
>AND BEING HAPPY
>IS
>BEING HAPPY
>IS
>BEING HAPPY *IS*...
>GOOD!!

2. The Ubus Make Plans

(**MA UBU** *and* **UBU** *eat Pixy Stix.*)

UBU. More.

MA UBU. That's enough.

(**UBU** *eats one more.*)

UBU. More.

MA UBU. That's enough.

(**UBU** *eats one more.*)

UBU. More!

MA UBU. That's –

UBU. Ma Ubu, you have to stop telling me things are enough.

Nothing is ever enough!

And that's why I'm king.

MA UBU. You're not king yet.

UBU. But I will be.

MA UBU. Mr. Wenz is the king. That's why they call him King Mr. Wenz.

And Rose Wenz is the queen. And that's why they call her Queen Mrs. Rose Wenz.

And if you killed them both, you could be king.

But right now, you're just eating Pixy Stix.

UBU. I'm making plans, you just can't see them.

MA UBU. Sugar prevents brain function. There have been studies.

Maybe that's why you haven't staged a successful government takeover yet and become the king.

UBU. I am amping myself up. Like famous athletes do.

(As if this is his idea.) And then I'm going to stage a successful government takeover and become the king!

MA UBU. You will?!

UBU. I just thought of it.

It was like a kind of epiphany, I guess you might call it.

MA UBU. I've been telling you to do that all week! And also a minute ago.

UBU. I don't remember that.

MA UBU. When are you going to do it?

UBU. Very soon.

MA UBU. And how?

UBU. Soon!

MA UBU. With what weapons?

UBU. Soon!

MA UBU. Have another Pixy Stick, Ubu. Have all the Pixy Stix.

UBU. I will!

>   *(He tears open Pixy Stix.)*
>
>   *(He throws them up in the air.)*
>
>   *(He shakes powdered colored sugar on and around himself in a frenzy.* **MA UBU** *watches him from the side.)*

MA UBU. My husband Ubu is kind of like a sheep dog. He just wants to shake his tail and shed everywhere and chase things. It doesn't even matter what things he's chasing. He could chase himself for miles and be perfectly happy.

I am not like a sheep dog.

I am like a shark.

>   *(Beat.)*

You might say that I can't become the king because Ubu will become the king.

And I would say to you: That's how much *you* know.

3. Royal Family Meeting

(The Wenz family has a meeting.)

(MR. WENZ, ROSE WENZ, WENZ JR., *and* **THE BABY WENZ.)**

MR. WENZ. Come to order, come to order.

We are going to have a Royal Family Meeting.

I will call roll.

The queen, my wife, Queen Mrs. Rose Wenz?

ROSE WENZ. Here!

MR. WENZ. Young Prince Wenz Jr.?

WENZ JR. Here.

MR. WENZ. The Baby?

THE BABY. Here.

MR. WENZ. Very good. We're all here. The Royal Family has met.

The first thing on today's agenda that I would like to discuss is the carpet in the rec room.

ROSE WENZ. What about it?

MR. WENZ. Somebody has been eating Doritos on that carpet.

If somebody keeps up this way, we will get ants and cockroaches and maybe mice.

ROSE WENZ. King Mr. Wenz, would you like to make a motion in this matter?

MR. WENZ. I would like to make a motion to ban Doritos in the rec room.

WENZ JR. Objection!

MR. WENZ. What is the objection?

WENZ JR. Doritos are tasty.

And tasty things are recreational.

And the rec room is for recreation.

(Beat. This is seriously considered.)

ROSE WENZ. Upheld.

MR. WENZ. Then I make a motion that Doritos must be eaten over plates in the rec room.

ROSE WENZ. Upheld.

WENZ JR. Upheld.

MR. WENZ. Upheld!

THE BABY. Doritos give you cancer.

(Pause.)

MR. WENZ. Excuse me?

THE BABY. I read an article. *Scientific American.*

MR. WENZ. Who has been letting The Baby read *Scientific American* again?

ROSE WENZ. Not me.

WENZ JR. Nope.

THE BABY. I ordered an online subscription and have been reading it late at night on my Kindle.

MR. WENZ. *Scientific American* is bad for you. You have to stop that at once.

THE BABY. How come?

ROSE WENZ. Reading is antisocial, Baby Wenz. You'll grow up warped and twisted and wrong and you'll be a cartoonist or a memoirist or a terrorist. So stop reading immediately.

MR. WENZ. Upheld.

WENZ JR. Upheld.

ROSE WENZ. Upheld.

What's the next item on our agenda?

THE BABY. I have an item.

ROSE WENZ. But...you're The Baby.

THE BABY. I know, but I have an item.

I was listening to NPR –

MR. WENZ. Who?

WENZ JR. What?

THE BABY. – And there was a report on the rising tides of fascism –

MR. WENZ. I make a motion that The Baby stops listening to NPR.

WENZ JR. Upheld.

THE BABY. But –

ROSE WENZ. I make a motion that The Baby just acts like a baby.

THE BABY. I just feel like the world is so fucked up! And I'm really worried about it.

Because by the time I'm an adult –

MR. WENZ. I make a motion that we invite our subjects and neighbors The Ubus over for dinner. And we can talk about Sports and we can talk about The Weather and we can talk about Reality Television Maybe, and The Baby can be socialized to be a baby.

ROSE WENZ. Upheld.

WENZ JR. Upheld?

THE BABY. I'm very concerned about this family.

4. The Wenzs and the Ubus Break Bread

(Kind of a dinner party.)

(All food and props are carefully mimed.)

(Except the Pixy Stix. They're real.)

*(The **UBUS** and **WENZS** sit on two benches.)*

MR. WENZ. We're so glad to have you over.

MA UBU. Thanks *so* much for having us.

>*(She kicks **UBU**.)*

UBU. A real pleasure!

ROSE WENZ. The pleasure is ours. Have some salad.

UBU. How nice! We love salad.

Is there any sugar?

>*(Beat.)*

ROSE WENZ. Sugar?

UBU. For the salad.

MA UBU. (Ubu!)

ROSE WENZ. Oh! Hmm...

UBU. Oh don't worry about it, it's fine.

>*(He takes out a Pixy Stick.)*

>*(He pours it directly into his mouth.)*

>*(The **WENZS** are horrified.)*

ROSE WENZ. *(Brightly.)* Well!

How is everybody doing? This weather has been lovely.

MR. WENZ. So warm!

MA UBU. *(Beaming.)* But cooling off at night.

ROSE WENZ. I love when it cools off at night! Then you can wear a sweater.

UBU. Pixy Stick, anyone?

EVERYBODY. No thank you.

UBU. You sure? Yum yum. Delish.

(Eats another.)

Like sunshine in a stick. Better than methamphetamines.

MR. WENZ. *(Jovial.)* Ha ha, Ubu, you're a funny man.

THE BABY. I think the FDA hasn't officially approved Pixy Stix, which means that they may not count as food items.

MA UBU. That's an adorable baby you all have!

ROSE WENZ. Thaaaaaank you (it's in a difficult age.)

MR. WENZ. Thaaaaaank you (it's just a baby.)

WENZ JR. It's gross, ugh, babies.

UBU. *(Brandishing a Pixy Stick.)* Live it up. Live on the edge. We can die at any minute. Shark? Airplane crash? Who knows! But right now, we're all here together. Yay! Community! Anybody?

MR. WENZ. *(Swayed.)* In the olden days the phrase for communal meals was "breaking bread." Isn't that great? That makes me nostalgic for times that have passed.

WENZ JR. *(Re: Pixy Stick.)* That looks cool.

ROSE WENZ. I guess this *is* a special occasion…

MA UBU. A special occasion indeed.

UBU. *(Distributing Pixy Stix.)* One for you

and one for you

and one for you

and one for you

and –

> *(He has gotten to* **MA UBU.***)*

I'm all out! We'll share.

Ready, set...bottoms up!!

> *(***MR. WENZ** *and* **ROSE WENZ** *and* **WENZ JR.** *toss back their Pixy Stix.* **THE BABY** *does not.)*
>
> *(They fall to the ground, dead.)*
>
> *(***THE BABY** *stares around him, horrified.)*

UBU. Poisoned Pixy Stix! I'm a genius!

MA UBU. Shh, we have a witness!

UBU. It's just a baby.

THE BABY. You just killed my entire family.

UBU. Here's the thing about family, my tiny friend. It comes and goes.

THE BABY. You just poisoned my entire family at family dinner.

UBU. The other thing about family is that it's kind of a fluid concept.

For example, *we* could be your family. Or if we left you in the field and you were raised by a group of friendly coyotes, they would be your family. Do you see what I'm getting at? Attachment is pain. But *fluid* attachment... is power.

THE BABY. But you see

the thing is

they were my family

and they invited you to dinner

and you killed them!

UBU. You're deliberately missing my point.

MA UBU. Should we knock it off too?

UBU. It's a baby.

MA UBU. Well I know that, but babies grow up into adults, and adults start revolutions and now that you are king, we can't have that.

UBU. Am I the king now?

> *(While this conversation happens,* **THE BABY** *gets up and sneaks out of the room.)*

MA UBU. Of course you're king!

UBU. Shouldn't there be a ceremony or certificate or a –?

MA UBU. All of that comes later, power comes first. But if you leave a mini-contender behind, you're unlikely to ever reap the rewards of your new position.

UBU. Okay, let's kill it.

> *(They turn around.* **THE BABY** *is gone.)*

MA UBU. Your first great mistake in office.

UBU. Children have poor memories. That one will grow up and move away and get a smartphone and all of this will be a distant dream.

5. The Baby Stays in a Hostel

(THE BABY.)

(It wears sunglasses. Maybe a Hawaiian shirt. Camera around the neck? Tourist-style.)

THE BABY. So after my parents and sibling were murdered at the dinner table, I grew up and decided to backpack the world for a while. The universe is a horrible and arbitrary place, and sometimes you just have to Do You.

So I bought a Lonely Planet Guide and a pair of Havaianas and some nice sunglasses and a new shirt, and now I am a Backpacker. And I find it very relaxing. The languages are always changing and so is the currency, and communication and money are both things that stress me out, so it's good to constantly be in situations where I can't be expected to understand either. Also, I've made a lot of casual friends, and I like having casual friends, so I can benefit from their company without being responsible for their well-being.

And if sometimes I think about what happened at my dinner table, and if – though I am filled with fury – I do nothing…I can't be blamed. I'm still on vacation.

6. Ubu in Charge

(**UBU** *sits in his throne.*)

(*His throne is a large bucket or metal tub. It is full of Pixy Stix sugar. He sits in it, like a kid in a sandbox. Occasionally he may dig out a handful of colored sugar and eat it.*)

UBU. Bring the next one in!

MA UBU. King Mr. Pa Ubu, may I introduce to you Subject Number Five, a Sad Postman.

(*She leads in a* **SAD POSTMAN**.)

SAD POSTMAN. Hello sir King Mr. Pa Ubu.

UBU. Kneel!!

(*The* **SAD POSTMAN** *looks at* **MA UBU**.)

MA UBU. He only talks when people kneel.

(*The* **SAD POSTMAN** *kneels.*)

SAD POSTMAN. Sir King Mr. Pa Ubu, I've come to you regarding the matter of a very large dog that always attacks me when I'm delivering the mail? And I've talked to the owners about it but they just say he's being playful, but he's not being playful.

UBU. Raise the taxes!

SAD POSTMAN. Excuse me?

UBU. Raise the taxes!

SAD POSTMAN. But...with all due respect, Sir King Mr. Pa Ubu, how does that help me?

MA UBU. (*Smoothly.*) The solution is to raise the taxes. Because then the owners will have to spend more on dog food, and it will be impossible to keep a very large dog, and instead they will have to get something much smaller that eats much less, like a parakeet or a guinea pig, and that won't be a bother at all when you deliver the mail.

SAD POSTMAN. But...I mean...do *I* have to pay more taxes?

UBU. Raise all the taxes!

MA UBU. Protection comes at a price. Thank you for coming all the way here. Let me show you out.

SAD POSTMAN. But...

>   (**MA UBU** *ushers him out.*)

>   (*Beat.* **UBU** *eats sugar.*)

MA UBU. (*Returning with a* **SAD TEACHER.**) Now introducing Subject Number Six, a Sad Teacher.

SAD TEACHER. Hello sir King Mr. Pa Ubu.

UBU. Kneel!!

>   (*The* **SAD TEACHER** *looks at* **MA UBU.**)

MA UBU. Yeah.

>   (*The* **SAD TEACHER** *kneels.*)

SAD TEACHER. Sir King Mr. Pa Ubu, I've come to you regarding the fact that there's no more money for education in this country, and we've run out of room in the budget for pens and pencils, so now my classes just sit out in the yard and draw with their fingers in the mud?

UBU. Raise the taxes!

SAD TEACHER. But is that going to...?

UBU. Tax the babies! Tax the first-graders! Tax the second, third, fourth, fifth, sixth-graders! Tax the high schoolers!

SAD TEACHER. But they don't...

UBU. Education comes at a price.

MA UBU. Thank you for coming all the way here. Let me show you out.

SAD TEACHER. But...

MA UBU. This way!

> (*She ushers the* **SAD TEACHER** *out.*)

> (*She turns back to* **UBU**.)

You can't keep raising the taxes.

UBU. Why not?

MA UBU. People don't like them and can't pay them and then they revolt.

UBU. I don't see anybody revolting. Except for you.

> (*He laughs at his own joke.*)

MA UBU. Listen, you have to raise the taxes when they aren't looking. You can't just say it to their faces.

UBU. This is hard work. I need a Pixy Stick.

> (*He eats a Pixy Stick.*)

MA UBU. Are you listening to me?

UBU. Bring in the next!

MA UBU. You're going to wish you'd listened to me.

UBU. NEXT!!

> (*A* **SAD DESTITUTE PERSON** *enters.*)

SAD DESTITUTE PERSON. Sir King Mr. Pa Ubu, I've come to you regarding the fact that I no longer have a home.

UBU. Oh, that one's easy. RAISE –

SAD DESTITUTE PERSON. Wait!!

I don't have anything. I can't afford a box. Actually, I just live inside a large paper bag.

(Beat. **UBU** *takes him in.)*

(Then finishes his yell:)

UBU. ...THE TAXES!!

SAD DESTITUTE PERSON. I'm going to tell everybody you're a terrible king.

They're all saying it quietly. But I'm going to say it the loudest. And people will hear me, and they'll come over to my bag to discuss how terrible you are, and there will be a revolution.

(Beat.)

MA UBU. King Mr. Pa Ubu, perhaps there's something we can do for this individual.

UBU. *(Very slowly, very clearly.)* I

declare

a

TAX

on

your

paper

BAG!

(Beat.)

(Of shock.)

*(***SAD DESTITUTE PERSON*** turns and walks out.)*

MA UBU. Ubu.

UBU. What.

MA UBU. You are mishandling things.

UBU. Don't tell me that I'm mishandling things! I'm sorry, are you the king? No? Well then go get the next subject so that I can continue being the king.

> (*Beat.*)
>
> (**UBU** *turns away.*)
>
> (**MA UBU** *bites back her rage.*)
>
> (*She goes to let the next subject in.*)

MA UBU. Next subject!

> (**HILLARY CLINTON** *enters.*)

HILLARY CLINTON. Hello?

MA UBU. Are you next in line?

HILLARY CLINTON. Oh. No. I'm here to see you.

MA UBU. Me!

> (*Takes a closer look.*)

Are you...?

You look like...

HILLARY CLINTON. Uh-huh.

MA UBU. ...Hillary Clinton?

HILLARY CLINTON. Hi.

MA UBU. Am I having a rage-fueled fantasy about female empowerment?

HILLARY CLINTON. I just want you to ask yourself if you are in your most-deserved position of power.

It's a question. You don't have to answer out loud. But I want you to ask yourself if you are doing the *most* that you can do to occupy the position that you deserve. Whatever that position is. I'm not saying it's king.

MA UBU. *(Owning this.)* I should be the king.

HILLARY CLINTON. I'm just asking questions.

And if the king is the position you *should* be in, I think what's clear is that you are *not* currently in that position.

MA UBU. How do we overthrow him?

HILLARY CLINTON. We?

UBU. *(Yelling.)* Ma Ubu! Where's the next subject?

MA UBU. You came to me in a rage-fueled fantasy. Aren't you here to help me?

HILLARY CLINTON. Sometimes when we ask questions, we already know the answers. And the questions are just tiny delays we give ourselves so that we don't have to know what we already know.

(She turns to go.)

MA UBU. Where are you going?

Are you coming back??

HILLARY CLINTON. Make me want to.

(She's gone.)

*(**MA UBU** stares after her. The whole world has shifted and changed and become a much more exciting place.)*

7. The Baby Meets an Old Friend

(The hostel. **THE BABY.** *He sunbathes.)*

*(***WENZ JR.** *enters. He has grown up, in the wake of his family tragedy. Now he's a lawyer.)*

WENZ JR. Hello?

THE BABY. The front desk is just inside, by the tiki torches.

WENZ JR. I'm looking for someone who's been staying here. A giant baby. Well, he's probably grown up by now, but his first name is The Baby, and his last name is Wenz.

THE BABY. *(Alarmed.)* And who's looking for him?

WENZ JR. His brother.

THE BABY. *You –?*

WENZ JR. Are *you* –?

(They embrace.)

THE BABY. I thought you were dead! Didn't you eat the poisoned Pixy Stick?

WENZ JR. I was out cold for a few days and when I woke up, I had a bad headache and everyone was gone. You look so different.

THE BABY. So do you!

WENZ JR. I went to a very prestigious and advanced law institute in Cambridge (Boston not England) and I got my JD. When you get your JD, you become an entirely different sort of person from the person you were previously. What have you been doing?

THE BABY. I've just been backpacking?

WENZ JR. Well, that's fun, and I'm glad you got a break. I'm here to fetch you, because we need to declare war.

THE BABY. War?

WENZ JR. While you've been hanging out in a hostel, the Ubus have been running our kingdom into the ground. Now the only thing you can buy anywhere is Pixy Stix! We have to take back what is rightfully ours.

THE BABY. Can we do this without a war?

WENZ JR. Do you really want to?

> *(Beat.* **WENZ JR.** *sees* **THE BABY**'s *hesitation and smiles.)*

My motorcycle is parked out front.

8. Ubu, Enchaîné

(**UBU**, *sad and alone. Locked in a very small space. We don't see the walls, we just see* **UBU** *in a tight box of light.*)

UBU. "They're having a sale," she said. "On Pixy Stix."

So I went to the store.

And then I got back and the locks had been changed and there was a big brawny bodyguard who hauled me away. And now here I am.

It's hard to be a man. In today's world. I don't know. We're supposed to be too many things at once. Stoic but expressive. Strong but vulnerable. Carefree but carefully styled. Is it my fault I overdid on one or a few of those things?

When I was a kid, I never wanted to be a leader. I just wanted to follow! I liked going to class and to the doctor and to the playground, because everybody always told me what to do when I got there. Then I grew up and everybody said: You have to lead! And I looked at people who were leading, and I did what they did. It was sort of my special trick – that I looked like a leader but I still got to follow.

Being a grownup is terrible. I don't know how any of us survive it.

9. Inside the War Room

> *(**MA UBU** and **HILLARY CLINTON** plan their strategy. There might be a large map spread out in front of them. Or a whiteboard. They are filled with elation as they stick Post-it Notes to the map.)*

MA UBU. And then we broker a diplomatic accord here.

And we encourage them to turn their aggressions... *there*.

And then while they're fighting, we take all their oil... from hence.

How's that sound?

HILLARY CLINTON. Great.

MA UBU. I feel great!

HILLARY CLINTON. Is your head all right?

MA UBU. My head?

HILLARY CLINTON. That crown looks so heavy. Maybe I just should hold it for a moment.

MA UBU. I'm okay.

HILLARY CLINTON. I wouldn't want you to get a headache.

MA UBU. I'm fine.

HILLARY CLINTON. Here, I'll hold it for you.

> *(Beat between them. That is maybe a little menacing?* **MA UBU** *opens her mouth...but before she can speak – there's a knock at the door.)*

MA UBU. Who is it?

(**THE BABY** *comes in. He may or may not carry a briefcase.*)

THE BABY. Ma Ubu?

(*Sees* **HILLARY CLINTON.**)

…Is that Hillary Clinton?

HILLARY CLINTON. Hi.

THE BABY. Oh cool. Hi.

(*Focusing!*)

I've come to deliver a contract, on behalf of Wenz Jr., of the mostly-deceased Wenz Family. Please read it, sign three copies, and return a single signed copy to me.

HILLARY CLINTON. Let's have a look.

(**THE BABY** *presents them with a contract.*)

MA UBU & HILLARY CLINTON. (*Reading out loud, in unison.*) The Wenz Family hereby subpoenas you ipso facto to the manner forthwith, and also involving, thereunto and thereby, the invitation to a war.

HILLARY CLINTON. Interesting.

MA UBU. When is the war?

THE BABY. Tomorrow.

MA UBU. Where is the war?

THE BABY. Wherever we are.

MA UBU. Don't wars take more work?

HILLARY CLINTON. Not always.

MA UBU. Well. Okay. That makes sense.

I'll sign.

(*She signs.*)

THE BABY. Thank you.

MA UBU. See you at the war!

10. On the Eve of Warfare

>(**THE BABY** *and* **WENZ JR.** *on the Eve of Warfare.*)

THE BABY. Brother?

WENZ JR. What is it?

THE BABY. What if...?

>I don't know...
>
>what if
>
>we didn't
>
>have
>
>a war?
>
>>*(Beat.)*

WENZ JR. Not...have a war?

THE BABY. ...Yeah.

WENZ JR. Like. Not...at *all?*

THE BABY. No...?

WENZ JR. Oh. Oh wow.

THE BABY. What if

>(if we didn't
>
>have a war)
>
>we could have
>
>other
>
>things?

WENZ JR. Like *what.*

THE BABY. Several small dogs?

>Or a lawn party?

WENZ JR. Oh *WOW*, okay.

No.

Stop.

I am going to teach you something, as your older brother and a male authority figure.

War is not this big scary thing.

War is not a grotesque moral failing.

War is the way adults have conversations.

THE BABY. ...It is?

WENZ JR. And what's more, every adult person knows that.

THE BABY. They do?

WENZ JR. Ma Ubu knows it.

I know it.

And now you know it.

THE BABY. I...

I guess

now I do.

WENZ JR. Okay! There we go!

> *(He holds up his hand. After a second,* **THE BABY** *gives him a high five.)*

Boom!

THE BABY. Boom.

WENZ JR. Welcome to adulthood.

11. The Great War

(What follows is a great war.)

(It might be underscored by a mighty piece of classical music. Or a great German opera.*)

(MA UBU and **HILLARY CLINTON** *enter. They carry Super Soakers filled with dye.)*

(THE BABY and **WENZ JR.** *enter. They do too.)*

(Beat: stand-off. They face each other.)

(They nod.)

(The war commences.)

(It is a free-for-all spectacular. It is a gorgeous and horrifying mess. Colored dye everywhere. Elaborate death scenes, after which somebody gets back up and keeps fighting. Imagine a cross between the war sequences in Platoon *and* Black Hawk Down...*and kids having a party. It should be fun and shocking and then occasionally genuinely disturbing.)*

(The war comes to an end.)

(THE BABY *is the only one left standing.)*

(A moment. And then **THE BABY** *raises his Super Soaker high into the air and does a savage, triumphant victory dance. It may be silent. It may not. It is the dance of a man who has discovered his purpose. It is the dance of a man, who was once a baby, who*

---

*A license to produce *Ubu Anew* does not include a performance license for any third-party or copyrighted music. Licensees should create an original composition or use music in the public domain. For further information, please see the Music and Third-Party Materials Use Note on page iii.

has had a taste of war…and is never going back.)

(The dance ends.)

(THE BABY *stands, dye-streaked chest heaving.)*

(HILLARY CLINTON *enters.)*

HILLARY CLINTON. Congratulations.

You won the war.

THE BABY. That was amazing!

This was the best war we could possibly have had!

I want everyone to come back and pick up their weapons

and then we can do this all over again!

Being an adult is AWESOME.

HILLARY CLINTON. That is a great attitude. That is a very positive attitude. I have a lot of hope for our next king.

THE BABY. Me?

HILLARY CLINTON. …Me.

But – you would make a delightful general.

THE BABY. General…?

HILLARY CLINTON. General The Baby Wenz.

THE BABY. I need another Super Soaker. I need several.

I need a confetti cannon.

(An epiphany.)

I need a credit card!

HILLARY CLINTON. You don't have a credit card?

THE BABY. I used to be a baby, so I didn't have one.

But then I grew up during the war.

And now I need a credit card.

HILLARY CLINTON. I think we can make that happen for you.

> *(They leave the battlefield, a united front.)*

> *(**MA UBU** enters, covered in colored dye, worse for wear. She has survived the war, because she survives everything. She is giving herself some tough love. [At no point does she cry.])*

MA UBU. So okay.

A war!

And okay, defeat, okay.

It happens!

It happens to the best of us.

It's just a little bit of defeat.

It's just a little bit of war.

What are you crying for.

> *(Slaps herself.)*

Stop crying!

> *(Slaps herself.)*

Stop crying!

> *(Slaps herself.)*

Stop crying!

> *(Straightens up.)*

Shape up.

Straighten up.

Lift your chin.

That's right.

Check your teeth.

Check your hair.

Check your rampant pessimism!

If you have a watch, check it.

If you have a bank account, check it.

If you have privilege, check it.

Okay.

Okay.

All our pieces are hither and thither.

All our bits were botched.

But we are gathering ourselves.

We are checking ourselves.

We are lying in wait like a coiled spring or an angry snake

or an unpaid bill or a rhinovirus

or a mother lion

or a mother other-lion

or a mother UBU!

And we will not concede defeat.

We only concede a brief setback.

> (**WENZ JR.** *walks onstage.*)
>
> (*He is also worse for wear, covered in dye.*)

WENZ JR. Oh how on earth did *you* survive.

MA UBU. Survive? I won!

WENZ JR. The Baby won, you didn't win.

MA UBU. There was a great war, and our forces clashed, and there was carnage, and I won.

That's the historical record that I've pieced together.

Who are you to question the historical record?

WENZ JR. Listen. You lost. And it seems like I lost. Even though I should have won. Because Hillary Clinton is king, and my brother is a general. And I have no position of power whatsoever.

(**MA UBU** *studies him.*)

MA UBU. Who are you again?

WENZ JR. Wenz Jr., poisoned Pixy Stix, etc.

MA UBU. Oh! That was a long time ago.

A lot has happened since then.

My memory isn't what it used to be.

No disrespect.

WENZ JR. Right.

(*Beat.*)

MA UBU. We could have another war.

WENZ JR. Sorry?

MA UBU. Sometime. I didn't mean right now. But I mean, another time, we could do that.

WENZ JR. What like, just you and me?

MA UBU. I mean I hadn't thought it through, I was just sort of thinking out loud, but you know, for example, say that Hillary Clinton and The Baby were traitors and had abandoned us both in cold blood and without any kind of advance warning – maybe there would be a situation in which you and I had another war – together – on the same side – for the purposes of defeating them.

(Beat.)

WENZ JR. You...and me?

MA UBU. It's just a thought.

WENZ JR. Interesting.

MA UBU. You think?

WENZ JR. You're full of surprises, Ma Ubu.

MA UBU. I just think –

So, let's say I killed your family. Just say that I did. Say that happened.

You can't take things personally, these days.

So you were my enemy five seconds ago. I can't take that personally!

The question is: what can we do for each other.

We're both adults here! We can both understand what is advantageous, and what is not advantageous! You know?

(A very thoughtful beat, and then...)

WENZ JR. I have a motorcycle parked just around the bend.

12. Ubu Sings a Song

(**UBU** *has avoided the entire war.*)

(*He has transformed his jail cell into kind of a hangout. He seems more relaxed than we've ever seen him. Calmer. Younger.*)

(*Perhaps there is a Giant Fish in a bowl.*)

UBU. I am still in jail alone, but that's fine! I used to be a very sad person. I used to think: I am a Failure. And then I realized: Here's the thing about failure. It hurts worse before than after. You see, now that everybody knows that I'm a loser, there's nothing to hide. No big secrets. Know what that feels like? Freedom.

(*Beat.*)

So now I'm raising fish. And I'm writing songs. And it's very peaceful in here.

I didn't like the outside world much anyway.

(**UBU** *sings a song for us.*)

(*Perhaps his Giant Fish sings with him.*)

["SONG ABOUT A GIANT FISH"]

WHEN I OBSERVE MY FISH AND THE WAY IT EATS FLAKES
I'M JUST LIKE CHAMPLAIN AS HE MAPPED THE GREAT LAKES
ITS DELICATE FINS ARE A REVELATION
ITS DAMP LITTLE NOSE IS A THRILLING SENSATION

WHEN I LOOK INTO THE GIANT EYES OF MY FISH
ITS UNBLINKING STARE GRANTS MY GREATEST LIFE-WISH
TO BE SEEN, TO BE KNOWN, TO BE NEVER ALONE
TO BE LOVED, TO BE OWNED, TO BE WHOLLY AT HOME.

FISH, YOU'RE A FISH! WHAT A FABULOUS FISH

I'D GO TO WAR FOR YOU, FABULOUS FISH
– IF I STILL WENT TO WAR – BUT I DON'T GO TO WAR!
I STAY HOME AND SPEND TIME WITH MY FISH

MY FISH IS A LEADER, IT TELLS ME TO FEED IT
MY FISH CALLS THE SHOTS, I DON'T HAVE TO LEAD IT
MY FISH HAS NO USE FOR WEALTH OR SUCCESS
AND FOR A FISH LIKE MY FISH, FAME DOESN'T IMPRESS.

FISH, YOU'RE A FISH! WHAT A FABULOUS FISH
I'D GO TO WAR FOR YOU, FABULOUS FISH
– IF I STILL WENT TO WAR – BUT I DON'T GO TO WAR!
I STAY HOME AND SPEND TIME WITH MY FIIIIIISH!

> *(A moment.)*
>
> *(Lights narrow down until they are focused on **UBU**.)*
>
> *(Beyond him, in the shadows, a wash of dye and sugar and destruction. Just beyond our view.)*
>
> *(Lights down.)*

End of Play

Your Mother in the Night Sky

YOUR MOTHER IN THE NIGHT SKY was commissioned by Montana Repertory Theatre under Artistic Director Michael Legg. It was written as an audio play and performed as part of the Plays On Call Festival, March 2021, directed by Michael Legg. The part of Your Mother was performed by Dale Raoul.

CHARACTERS

YOUR MOTHER – Talkative, cheerful, makes friends easily. Underneath that, a real sadness that she does her best to keep from you, because you don't like it.

AUTHOR'S NOTES

This is a voicemail. The strangest voicemail you've ever received.

(*) is where the voicemail cuts off. Then your mother calls you back.

In the background: a strange soundscape. A low, pervasive hum that does not obscure your mother's words, but makes it sound like she's calling from inside the heart of a large machine.

While this was originally written as an audio play, it would also work onstage.

YOUR MOTHER. Hi honey, this is your mother

and

the *strangest* thing just happened to me, I –

(hang on a second)

> *(The background sound intensifies, then reduces, as if she's stepping away into a quieter space.)*

OK it's me again, sorry

hmm I'm trying to think how to tell you this but

I *did* just want to call because

I told you I'd call and I didn't want you to worry and

actually I think I'm late by now

I might be an hour late or

a few days late? I don't know how much time has passed in here

but I hope you didn't wait up

I hope you weren't worried.

I'm all right, so please don't worry about that, but

this is just the oddest experience I've ever had and I feel that I should tell someone.

I thought about telling someone other than you

(for obvious reasons)

but...

> *(Pause. This is dangerous territory between you and **YOUR MOTHER**. You have always accused her of exaggerating. It hurts her feelings because she doesn't think she exaggerates, she just thinks she tells things a little better than she found them.)*

I'm in a big – vessel.

I think it's a vessel.

I was picked up last night –

I was driving home from book club – to call *you* actually –

and as I came over the hill, there was a big light right in front of me, on the road,

hovering

(at the time I thought it was very powerful headlights

truck headlights? but high off the ground so

maybe I didn't think they were headlights)

anyway it was all very sudden and I braced for a collision of some kind

and then...I was here.

Waking up.

In this sort of...belly. Like a mechanical belly. And

I've seen the people who brought me here

(I know how this sounds, honey, so I don't want you to

get the way you can get but)

they are very small and sort of

green-gray skinned

greeny-gray

like a lizard

not unpleasant

(they've been *very* polite)

but the strangest thing of all –

*

Hi it's me again, your mother, calling back

(I got cut off)

I still seem to have signal, which is odd because I think we're in orbit

of the earth, I think we're orbiting the earth,
but I guess there are a *lot* of cell-phone towers and
Verizon satellites? do they have satellites?
Anyway,

I woke up and it was explained to me
(not with words, but with – images, sort of)
that they're just doing a few minor experiments
and they asked if I wanted anything
and I was worried about you, about not having called you
and I guess they could see that
because one of them sort of rifled in its...pouch?
(like a scaly frontal pouch they seem to have?)
and brought out my cell phone.
So then I called you.

Uh. I feel like I was going to... What was I...?
Oh yes! "The strangest thing of all."

I was talking to the lizard that seems to be the captain or...leader?
and they expressed to me that they were happy to be back
on Earth, in the neighborhood of Earth
and I said, "What do you mean back?"
and they said, oh, they were here sort of a while ago
they did some work on these big stone triangles in a desert,
and I said, "Do you mean the pyramids?"
and they got really excited, they asked if I knew their work

and I said, you know, I've seen *pictures*, I can't say that I've ever *been*
and they said –

*

Hi. Me again. I think maybe when we're between satellites I lose you?
Anyway.
In short, there are a lot of lizard people on the planet.
Oh that sounded rude –
I don't really know what to call them
I don't want you to think they look like lizards but
if you were just...at a glance, in passing –
you could be confused.
Anyway:
postal workers!
There are a lot of postal workers who are their kind
(because they're so good with systems, with organizational systems)
also neurosurgeons
also architects!
also...oh who else did they say?
They said somebody famous
but I don't think I should say it over the phone
(It was surprising, though!)

And they said they just, they all have these *suits*
that look like us
you have to wear them for forty-eight hours before you go down
it's like a suit of spray-on skin
and it takes forty-eight hours for the skin to become pliable enough that it just

molds itself to your body, and fills out human-shape where you're a different shape

and they said it takes about forty-eight hours to get off, too

if you ever need to take it off

it's really sticky and unpleasant, there's this whole chemical bath involved.

Isn't that cool? I had no idea!

They said that they have friends who have stayed in the suit for *decades*

and they know friends of friends who lived lifetimes in the suit

and died in the suit

and *that* is...commitment.

I was impressed by that.

Things haven't been easy for me, as you know, and

I've never said this to you, but lately they've been harder, and

I've been tempted to just...give up.

But to spend *decades* in a spray-on suit

to spend a *lifetime* in a human suit

even when it's hard, or you're tired, or you're lonely...

I find that really inspiring.

I thought you might be inspired by that as well since

I would never call you *lazy*, sweetheart, but

you really don't push yourself as hard as you –

*

(This time when she calls back, the soundscape has changed. There's a kind of rhythmic, mechanical pulsing, and a very faint but oddly choral sound in the background. A

> *collective chirping, or collective vocal hum. However you achieve it, the impression is of a great many beings who have gathered for a task, and the task is getting underway.)*

Hello, it's your mother,

again.

I actually need to go pretty soon, Pyramid just said that the experiment is about to start –

but don't worry, they said it wouldn't hurt at all.

They said to think of it like an upgrade, getting an upgrade

And then their friend said to think of it like going to the salon

and then a third one said to think of it like an amusement park ride?

Which struck me as odd

but

either way it sounds like everything will be fine

and they're all so *nice*, I really feel like I've made some friends.

So, I'll probably be home soon and

if you'd just stop by my place and make sure the cats are okay

that would be lovely

and I think I had a load in the dryer, it's probably all wrinkled

but you could take it out for me

(you could even fold it!)

> *(The chanting/humming/task-in-progress sound is growing louder.)*
>
> *(A sudden burst of urgency – this comes from a place of truth and raw love that* **YOUR**

MOTHER *doesn't often feel she can access when she's speaking to you:)*

– and I just want to say that you haven't always been a *good* child

but you've been the best one for me.

OK.
OK, that's all now.
Bye.

Real American Dinner Party

REAL AMERICAN DINNER PARTY in its current version was recorded as an audio play by Playing On Air under Producing Artistic Director Claudia Catania. It was directed by Rachel Chavkin, and the cast was as follows:

MARCY .... Quincy Tyler Bernstine
SAIDEE .... April Matthis
THOM .... Sean Carjaval
GRANT .... Matthew Rauch

An earlier version of *REAL AMERICAN DINNER PARTY* was commissioned by Single Carrot Theatre under Artistic Director Genevieve de Mahy. It was produced in April 2017 and directed by Dustin C.T. Morris.

CHARACTERS

MARCY – (female, early twenties) Mousy, easily intimidated, trying so hard to please.

SAIDEE – (female, late twenties) Her sister, who does not approve of her life choices. They are always competing.

THOM – (male, late twenties) Saidee's boyfriend, affable and non-confrontational. He wants everybody to think he's a nice guy.

GRANT – (male, early forties) Marcy's boyfriend, rich, pushy. He doesn't respect her.

AUTHOR'S NOTES

Set: Fancy stuffed chairs, a small table, drinks, glasses. Posh but minimal. Thrillingly ugly taxidermy if possible.

Tone: The first four pages should feel like a hyper-realistic play about American Upper-Class Family Tension. When the play turns, it turns with a vengeance.

Casting: Characters can be played by actors of any race, ethnicity, and gender identity.

Also: Every compliment should feel subtly double-edged. None of these people respect each other, but to reveal one's hand too baldly is to lose the game.

(MARCY, SAIDEE, THOM, and GRANT have drinks in Saidee and Thom's new apartment.)

GRANT. It's great. It's a great place.

MARCY. I just love it. Your place is just lovely.

THOM. Oh, it's not really...

SAIDEE. It's just a place.

MARCY. No, it's lovely. You have views. There are views.

GRANT. Got a lot of space. Looks like you got some space. Great first apartment.

MARCY. And a yard. You have a yard! I've been saying to Grant –

GRANT. *(Re: terrible piece of kitsch.)* And that. What's that.

THOM. Oh, it's just a little –

SAIDEE. It's ironic.

MARCY. *(Very brightly.)* That's funny! That's so funny! It's such a playful –

GRANT. *(Cutting her off.)* I don't think irony has a place in interior décor, but that's me.

Was that a billiards table I saw in the back? You play billiards?

THOM. Oh, on occasion.

SAIDEE. He does, he does play billiards.

THOM. I'm not very good.

SAIDEE. He's very good.

THOM. Just have some friends over, you know. A few drinks, you know.

SAIDEE. He always wins, when he plays.

MARCY. Grant plays too. He's very good, too.

GRANT. I'm pretty good. I'm decent.

MARCY. Grant is good at sports, in general.

SAIDEE. Oh I wouldn't call pool a sport.

MARCY. *(An edge.)* Billiards, it's billiards. It's basically a sport.

(Pause.)

GRANT. I played football back in the day.

(To **THOM.** *)* You play some football?

THOM. I never did. All that...impact.

MARCY. The NFL courted him.

SAIDEE. Evidently he took a different path.

MARCY. Grant had lots of paths open to him. He has a lot of...expertise.

SAIDEE. Well he's had a lot more *time*. Than the rest of us.

THOM. The NFL. That's fabulous.

MARCY. *(With a tight smile.)* Grant isn't old.

GRANT. *(Enjoying how effeminate the word is.)* "Faaabulous."

SAIDEE. I didn't say he was old.

THOM. *(Trying to find a more manly word.)* Awesome? Great!

GRANT. "Faaabulous."

SAIDEE. *(To* **GRANT.** *)* I've heard so much about you. Marcy loves to call home and talk about you.

GRANT. *(Unaware of the tension, or ignoring it.)* She's a great girl. She was a great secretary.

MARCY. Oh, not really. I wasn't anything special, really.

GRANT. Well, you couldn't type and you jammed the copier, but you had a great ass.

> *(He laughs, they don't.* **THOM** *sort of laughs, an after-the-fact, half-hearted laugh.)*

MARCY. *(Embarrassed but trying to act cool.)* Oh now, honey.

GRANT. *(Still reminiscing.)* You always burned the coffee though.

Guess you were a pretty bad secretary.

SAIDEE. *(Pointed.)* How's the job search coming, anyway?

MARCY. Oh, well.

SAIDEE. Yes?

MARCY. You know.

SAIDEE. *(Won't drop it.)* Uh-huh?

MARCY. Well, it's sort of on hold. I've put it on hold.

GRANT. *(To* **THOM**.*)* I don't think she needs to be out there on the *streets*. Pounding the *pavement*.

SAIDEE. On "hold."

MARCY. You know, I'm so busy, I've been so busy, moving in with Grant kept me so busy...

GRANT. What kind of a man would I be if I couldn't provide for my girl?

MARCY. Oh now...

SAIDEE. So it's "on hold."

MARCY. There's just so much to do...unpacking...and... uh...unpacking, and...

GRANT. I mean hey! You know? Ain't like we need any extra, with what I make.

    (Laughs.)

You know?

    (To **THOM.***) You* know.

SAIDEE. I work. Thom works, and I work.

GRANT. You're young. You're kids. You'll see.

    (To **THOM.***)* You get older, you won't want your girl out there on the streets.

SAIDEE. *(To* **MARCY.***)* Were you out on the streets?

MARCY. *(Loud whisper.)* Saidee.

SAIDEE. *(Normal volume.)* What.

MARCY. *(Loud whisper.)* Saidee!

SAIDEE. *(Normal volume.)* No, I'm just asking, I'm having a nice dessert with my sister and her boyfriend and I'm asking if my sister has been spending her pre-boyfriend years out on the *streets*, that's all. Is there a problem?

GRANT. What's the problem?

SAIDEE. Exactly, what's the problem?

    (Then **THOM**'s *eyeball falls out.)*

    (He clasps a hand to his eye.)

THOM. Oh!

SAIDEE. What's wrong.

THOM. My eyeball fell out.

SAIDEE. Your –?

THOM. My eyeball! Fell out.

MARCY. Oh!

SAIDEE. *All* the way out?

THOM. All the way. Out. It rolled. Ow. Don't anybody step on it.

GRANT. All right! Okay! Everybody just freeze! I got this under control!

SAIDEE. I'm on it. We're on it.

(*She and* **GRANT** *look.*)

THOM. My doctor said I should get glasses. Sometimes I squint too hard, and then I get eye strain, and he said that someday I would just squint my eye right out of my socket. And I guess that day was today.

MARCY. (*To* **SAIDEE**, *a little triumphant.*) That's awful.

GRANT. Got it! I got it!

THOM. You got it?

SAIDEE. That's a grape. Grant?

That's a grape.

GRANT. Oh.

MARCY. That – what's that right there.

SAIDEE. That's a dustball, Marcy. I haven't spent every waking hour of my life cleaning Thom's apartment for him, so that's a dustball.

MARCY. Grant's allergic to dust.

THOM. (*Getting more stressed.*) Does anybody see my eyeball?

SAIDEE. We're going to find it, honey, don't freak out.

THOM. I'm not "freaking out," I just don't want anybody to step –

SAIDEE. Nobody is stepping on it, Thom, I said I'm looking –

THOM. Yes but you don't look where you're going, you never look –

SAIDEE. Oh, *I* never look –?

MARCY. She *doesn't* really look, when we were growing up she never –

SAIDEE. Like *either* of you have any sort of *awareness* of –

MARCY. What's that supposed to –

THOM. Can you guys just please –

SAIDEE. OH!

THOM. Did you find it?

SAIDEE. *(One hand to her eye.)* My eyeball fell out.

THOM. What?

MARCY. No!

GRANT. I think it rolled that way.

SAIDEE. Did you see it? Can you –?

GRANT. Hang on – yeah – it definitely sort of rolled in that –

THOM. Okay, but what about my –

GRANT. *(Hands and knees, searching.)* Is this, right here –?

THOM & SAIDEE. Yes!

GRANT. *(Picks it up.)* I think it's another grape –

Ooh. Oop. No. It's squishy.

THOM & SAIDEE. DON'T SQUISH IT.

GRANT. Whose is it?

THOM & SAIDEE. MINE!

MARCY. Well, what color is it?

GRANT. I don't know, it's dusty. It has dust all over it.

MARCY. *(To* **SAIDEE.***)* You really should dust, people are allergic to dust.

SAIDEE. *(To* **GRANT.***)* My eye definitely rolled in that direction –

THOM. That eye was closer to me, and mine looks more –

SAIDEE. – It looks smaller, like it would fit my face better –

GRANT. *(Hand over his eye.)* Oh!

SAIDEE. Oh no!

GRANT. My eye's gone!

THOM. *(Gesturing toward the dusty eyeball.)* Can you just hand me that...?

GRANT. *(To* **MARCY.***)* Do something!

Do something!

My eye fell out, Marcy!

Why are you just sitting there?

Marcy?

Marcy!

MARCY!

> *(Both of* **MARCY***'s eyes have fallen out somewhere during the fuss.)*
>
> *(She sits aloof. Very calm.)*
>
> *(A moment of quiet empowerment.)*

MARCY. Both my eyes fell out, Grant.

So I can't see where your eye went.

I can't even see you at all, so I'm sorry, but I can't help you.

> **(GRANT, SAIDEE,** *and* **THOM** *freeze. Lights dim on them. They recede from* **MARCY***'s*

consciousness, in a way, while **MARCY** *is alone in a strange silence.)*

MARCY. And then from the dark caves of my wet and empty sockets,

a vision reflected back at me.

All the things that I always have to look at – day after day after day –

like Grant's jaw…and Grant's hair…and Grant's frown…

were suddenly gone.

So I could finally see.

And I saw a city.

A yellow wind blew trash through the streets.

Puddles of standing water in the gutters.

I was walking down that street.

It was not a clean street, but I was on it nonetheless

and so, perhaps, it was *my* street.

Not the one I would have chosen

but the one I was on.

Alone, yes.

But not lonely.

Moving in a forward sort of direction.

(A real beat. She looks at us. A sober, penetrating stare that is deeply unsettling.)

And so I went forward.

Unflinchingly forward.

And then I was gone.

(Beat.)

(Lights down.)

End of Play

www.ingramcontent.com/pod-product-compliance
Lightning Source LLC
Chambersburg PA
CBHW072014290426
44109CB00018B/2236